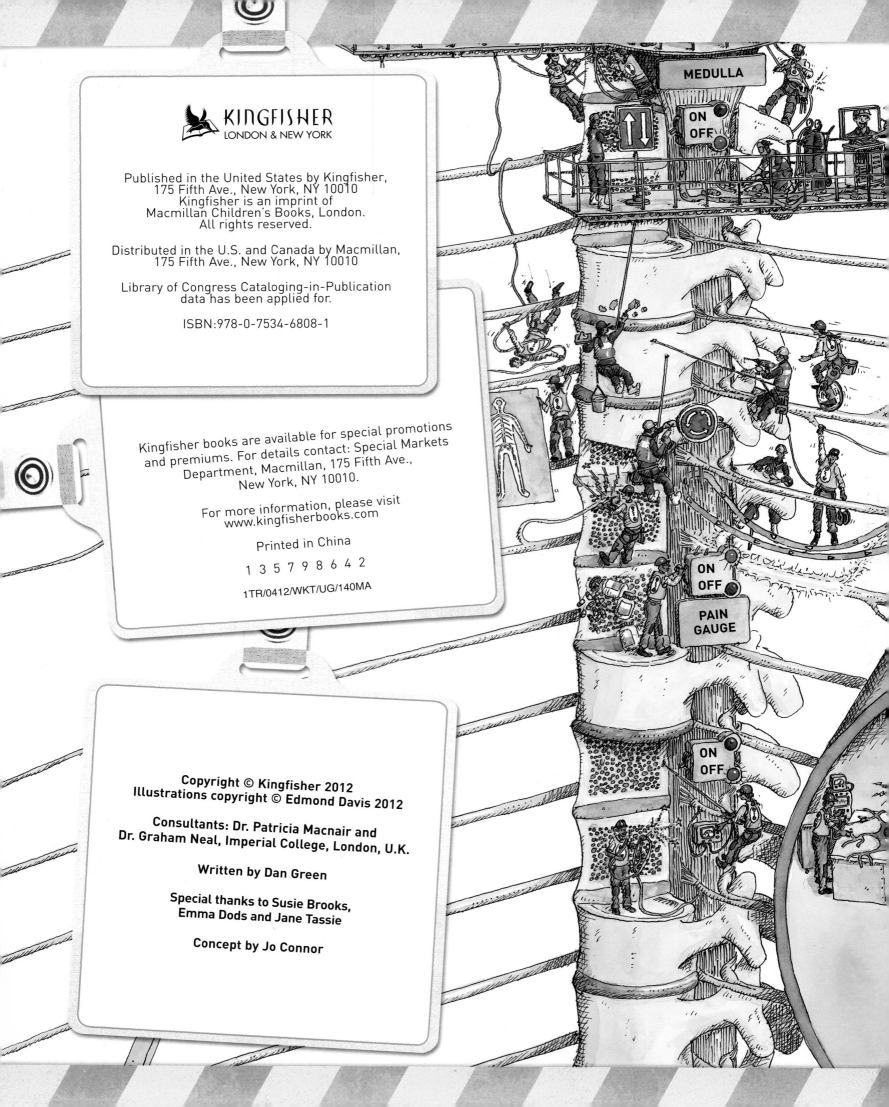

KINGFISHER
LONDON & NEW YORK

Published in the United States by Kingfisher,
175 Fifth Ave., New York, NY 10010
Kingfisher is an imprint of
Macmillan Children's Books, London.
All rights reserved.

Distributed in the U.S. and Canada by Macmillan,
175 Fifth Ave., New York, NY 10010

Library of Congress Cataloging-in-Publication
data has been applied for.

ISBN:978-0-7534-6808-1

Kingfisher books are available for special promotions
and premiums. For details contact: Special Markets
Department, Macmillan, 175 Fifth Ave.,
New York, NY 10010.

For more information, please visit
www.kingfisherbooks.com

Printed in China

1 3 5 7 9 8 6 4 2

1TR/0412/WKT/UG/140MA

Copyright © Kingfisher 2012
Illustrations copyright © Edmond Davis 2012

Consultants: Dr. Patricia Macnair and
Dr. Graham Neal, Imperial College, London, U.K.

Written by Dan Green

Special thanks to Susie Brooks,
Emma Dods and Jane Tassie

Concept by Jo Connor

Contents

Don't forget to inspect the amazing Human Body Factory poster!

Introduction

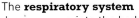

YOU ARE HERE

Welcome to the Human Body Factory! You're about to take a wild roller-coaster tour of the cranking, sloshing, pumping parts that keep you alive and kicking! Discover each part of your body as a busy department, packed with wacky workers and manic machines. To check where you are in the body, look for the red dot on a figure like this in the introduction tag.

The **respiratory system** draws oxygen into the body and removes carbon dioxide gas. Air shoots in through the mouth or nose and continues to the **lungs**, which pass the oxygen over to the blood.

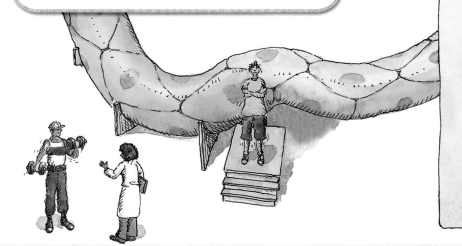

Each division of the Human Body Factory works nonstop to do its job—there's no opportunity for a vacation around here! The different departments clunk and churn in their own ways, but they all need one another to keep the body healthy. They come together in **ten major body systems**.

The **immune system** keeps the works healthy and infection-free, using killer cells and chemical weapons. It's given a helping hand by the **skin, hair, and nails**, which wrap the body in a protective casing. Meanwhile, the **endocrine system** monitors how body cells work and change, affecting how fast we burn energy and how we grow and develop.

IMMUNE CELLS

Neutrophil Blasts bacteria and fungi

Eosinophil Targets larger parasites and activates allergic response

Basophil Triggers allergic response

Monocyte Mops up dead cells

T cell Fights viruses and cancer cells

B cell Memorizes ways of making antibodies

Mast cell General protection close to the skin

The **cardiovascular system** sends **blood** to all parts of the body, using the **heart** to pump it around. The blood takes deliveries to all the body's cells, and carries away their waste including taking carbon dioxide to the lungs.

The **mouth**, **stomach,** and **intestines** mash up food in the **digestive system**. With some help from the **liver**, they get at the good stuff and circulate it in the blood. Any leftovers leave the body as poop.

Waste that builds up in the blood is filtered by the **kidneys** and turned into pee by the **urinary system**. It gets stored for a while in the **bladder** before leaving the body for good.

EXIT

The **reproductive system** manages the planning and construction of new human units.

HEAD OFFICE

So, are you ready to slide down arteries and splash around the stomach? Look out for the gnashing, grinding mouth—and don't get stuck in the boogers at the nose station! Along the way, keep a sharp eye out for Clatterbones, the skeleton. He's hiding throughout the book and you can award yourself a brain cell each time you spot him!

The **nervous system** is led by Head Office—the **brain**. It monitors what's going on inside and outside of the body, and sends messages along the **nerves** to operate the **musculoskeletal system** so that the body can move.

COME ON, DON'T WAIT ANY LONGER . . .

The Brain

YOU ARE HERE

The Human Body Factory would be chaos without its Head Office—the brain! This bossy department controls all of the body's movements and also generates thoughts, dreams, and memories and boasts problem-solving powers. It works using nerve cells called neurons, which zap signals between each other at lightning speed.

Thalamus
Hypo-thalamus
Olfactory bulb (smell)
Cerebellum
Cerebral cortex
Hippo-campus
Amygdala

The outer layer of the brain is the **cerebral cortex**. It looks like a wrinkly walnut, but there are other parts hidden inside!

Come on, **thalamus** team—let's get these sense signals from the nervous system to the correct parts of the brain.

*It's the **neuron** cell bodies that do all of the main brain work. They form an outer layer called **gray matter**. Underneath, in the **white matter**, fibers link the neurons together.*

Feeling moody? Blame the **hypothalamus**. We work closely with the endocrine system (see pages 16–17).

*Now where did I put those old memories? In the **hippocampus** we make sure the boss remembers things!*

Each half, or **hemisphere**, of the brain handles slightly different tasks. One half is always more bossy than the other. It dictates whether a person is left- or right-handed.

*H-E-L-P! The **amygdala** is the area that holds our deepest fears.*

Right brain
Left side of body
Visual imagery and music
Facial recognition
3-D awareness

Left brain
Right side of body
Language
Verbal skills
Logical tasks and math

The brain guzzles a lot of energy and oxygen. We supply these in the blood, through a giant loop of **blood vessels**.

*Shh, I'm trying to concentrate! In the **reticular formation** we "fade out" distractions. We also turn the brain off or on when it's time to sleep or wake up.*

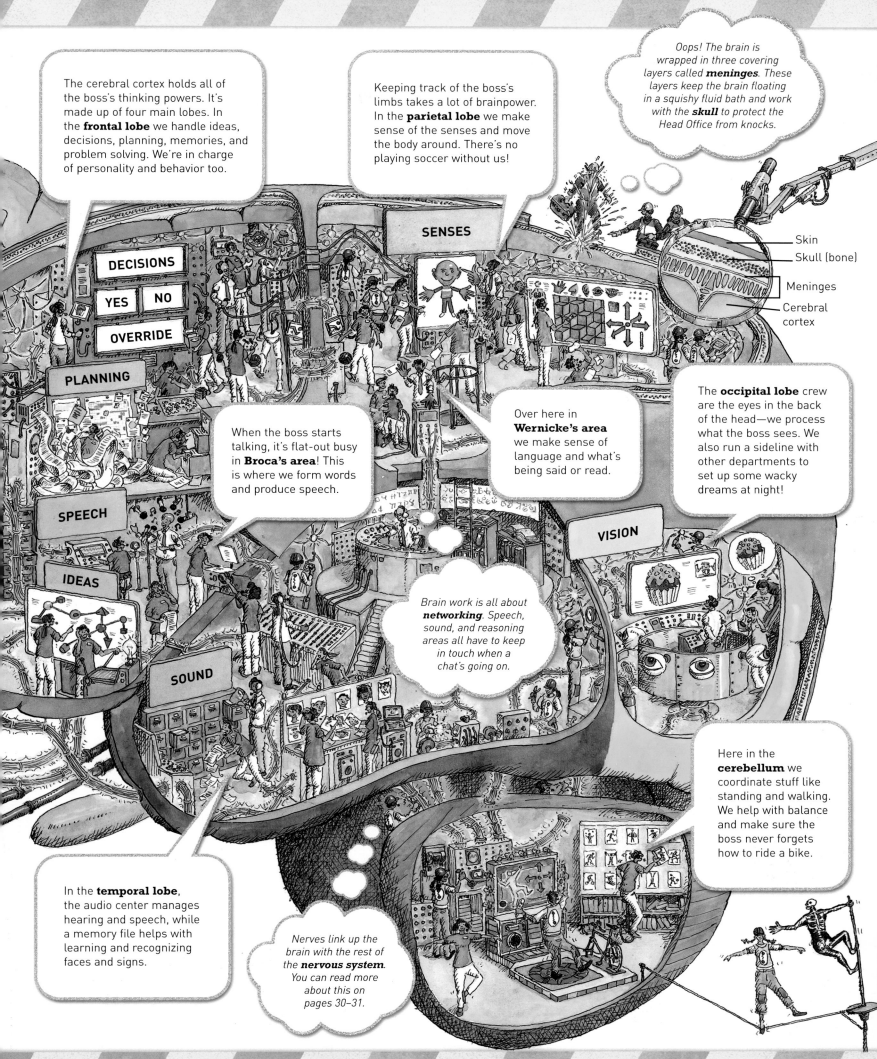

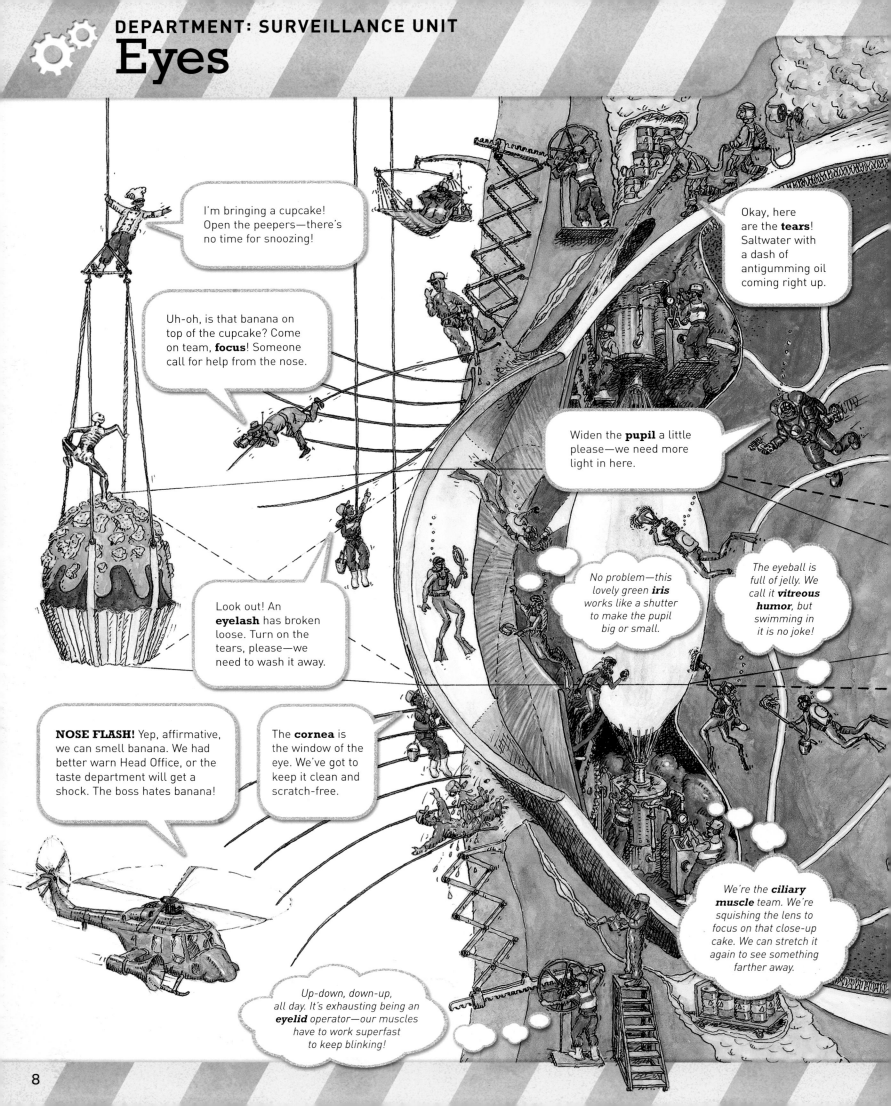

Heave ho! **Muscles** at the ready to swivel the eye upward.

Let's get these broken **rods and cones** replaced. We need cone cells for color vision and rod cells for low-light vision.

The eyes are the spy hubs of the Body Factory! They work just like two cameras, taking in light and creating pictures for the body to see. Special lenses bend the light and focus it onto sensitive nerve cells. These cells zap signals to the brain, which decodes them to make sense of what's in sight.

YOU ARE HERE

The **retina** lines the back of the eye. Its most sensitive spot, the **fovea centralis**, is packed with cone cells.

Message from the **brain** to the six outer eye muscles: please swivel carefully to focus on that cupcake. Up a bit, left a bit, down a bit . . . that's it. Oh dear—definitely banana!

ROD & CONE REPAIR

E
F P
T D Z

Hey, you're blocking the light beams, silly. That's not a real cupcake—it's just an **upside-down image**! The brain will turn it the right way up.

Ah, the **blind spot**—no rods or cones here.

The **optic nerve** flashes signals from the retina back to the brain. Check the wires carefully—we've got to keep them operating at high speed.

So you see . . . detailed information from both of your eyes is combined inside the brain . . .

. . . and what you get is a perfect 3-D image. Seeing is believing!

eyes   crossing of nerves

brain

Ears

I wonder if they can hear me tuning my tuba . . . PARP!

This outer part of the ear—the **pinna**—is like a big collecting dish. It gathers sounds and channels them into the earhole. The two ears work together to pick up sounds from all around.

YOU ARE HERE

The Wiretap and Audio Recon unit operates the sophisticated "parts" of the ear. It keeps the body aware of its surroundings and its position in space. This department has three zones—the outer ear collects sounds; the middle ear passes on the vibrations; and the inner ear translates them into nerve signals for the brain. The inner ear also helps with balance.

No fooling around once you've entered the **earhole**. It's slippery inside—and noisy. Keep your shoes and ear protectors on at all times.

Hey, this is the **eye** department speaking! Can you lend us an ear up here? I see people playing music, but the boss wants to know if they're playing his favorite tune!

Actually, the ear canal cleans itself automatically—we're just helping. **Wax** traps any dirt and dust, and then **microscopic hairs** brush it out toward the earhole.

Oops, missed! I'm trying to keep the **ear canal** clear so that **sound waves** can travel along it.

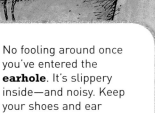

FACTORY BAND LUNCHTIME REHEARSALS

*It's easy to pierce the **earlobe**, because it doesn't have any bone or cartilage in it.*

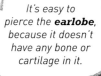

NOISE METER	DECIBELS (DB)	
	Jet engine	130
	Loud music	110
	Shouting	70
	Talking	50
	Whisper	20
	Silence	0

Aaagh, something's not right—I feel dizzy!

Straighten up, please! These **semicircular canals** monitor the body's position using tiny hair cells that track liquid sloshing back and forth. They send signals to the **cerebellum**, the part of the brain that deals with standing upright and balancing.

HEAD OFFICE

The eardrum vibrates against the **malleus** bone, which jiggles the **incus**, which rattles the **stapes**—the smallest bone in the body. Together, these bones are called the **ossicles**.

Brain tuning in . . . wow, this band rocks! Let's **filter** out the background noise—I don't like the sound of that tuba.

SSSH! NO LOUD NOISES

This spiral bone is called the **cochlea**. It's full of fluid— and 30,000 microscopic hairs. Vibrations from the ossicle bones make tiny ripples in the fluid. The hairs turn these into electrical pulses, which are sent down **nerve** wires to the brain.

Sound level's good and clear! What you hear depends on how sound waves **vibrate** the air. Large vibrations make loud sounds, and speedy vibrations make high-pitched sounds.

I'm getting great vibes from the **eardrum**. This thin, springy membrane is stretched tight, like a rubber sheet. Sound waves make it vibrate— and really loud sounds can damage it.

Loudness is measured on the **decibel scale**. We can't hear sounds below 0 decibels. Anything higher than 150 decibels is likely to burst your eardrums. OUCH!

Whew, we just made it through! The **eustachian tube** opens when the mouth yawns to keep **pressure** inside the ear even. It lets out air and **mucus** from the middle ear and sends it to the back of the throat.

TO THROAT

Nose

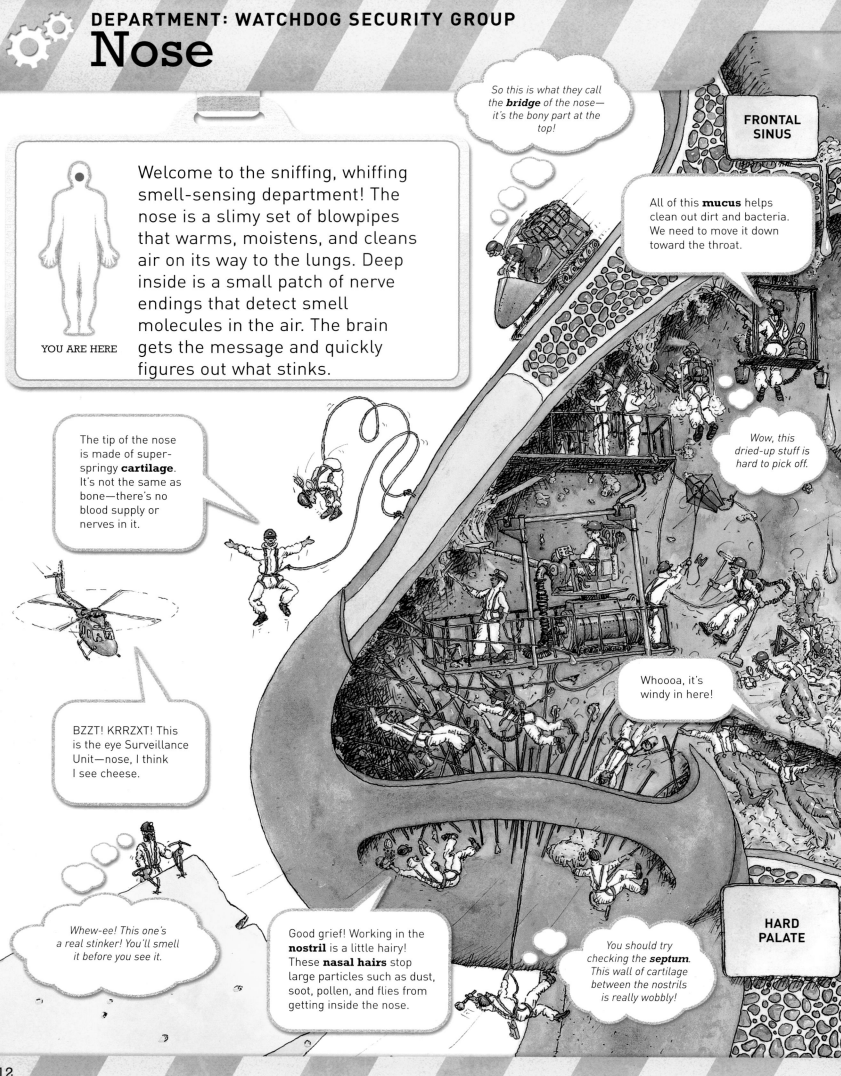

YOU ARE HERE

Welcome to the sniffing, whiffing smell-sensing department! The nose is a slimy set of blowpipes that warms, moistens, and cleans air on its way to the lungs. Deep inside is a small patch of nerve endings that detect smell molecules in the air. The brain gets the message and quickly figures out what stinks.

So this is what they call the **bridge** of the nose—it's the bony part at the top!

FRONTAL SINUS

All of this **mucus** helps clean out dirt and bacteria. We need to move it down toward the throat.

Wow, this dried-up stuff is hard to pick off.

The tip of the nose is made of super-springy **cartilage**. It's not the same as bone—there's no blood supply or nerves in it.

BZZT! KRRZXT! This is the eye Surveillance Unit—nose, I think I see cheese.

Whoooa, it's windy in here!

Whew-ee! This one's a real stinker! You'll smell it before you see it.

Good grief! Working in the **nostril** is a little hairy! These **nasal hairs** stop large particles such as dust, soot, pollen, and flies from getting inside the nose.

You should try checking the **septum**. This wall of cartilage between the nostrils is really wobbly!

HARD PALATE

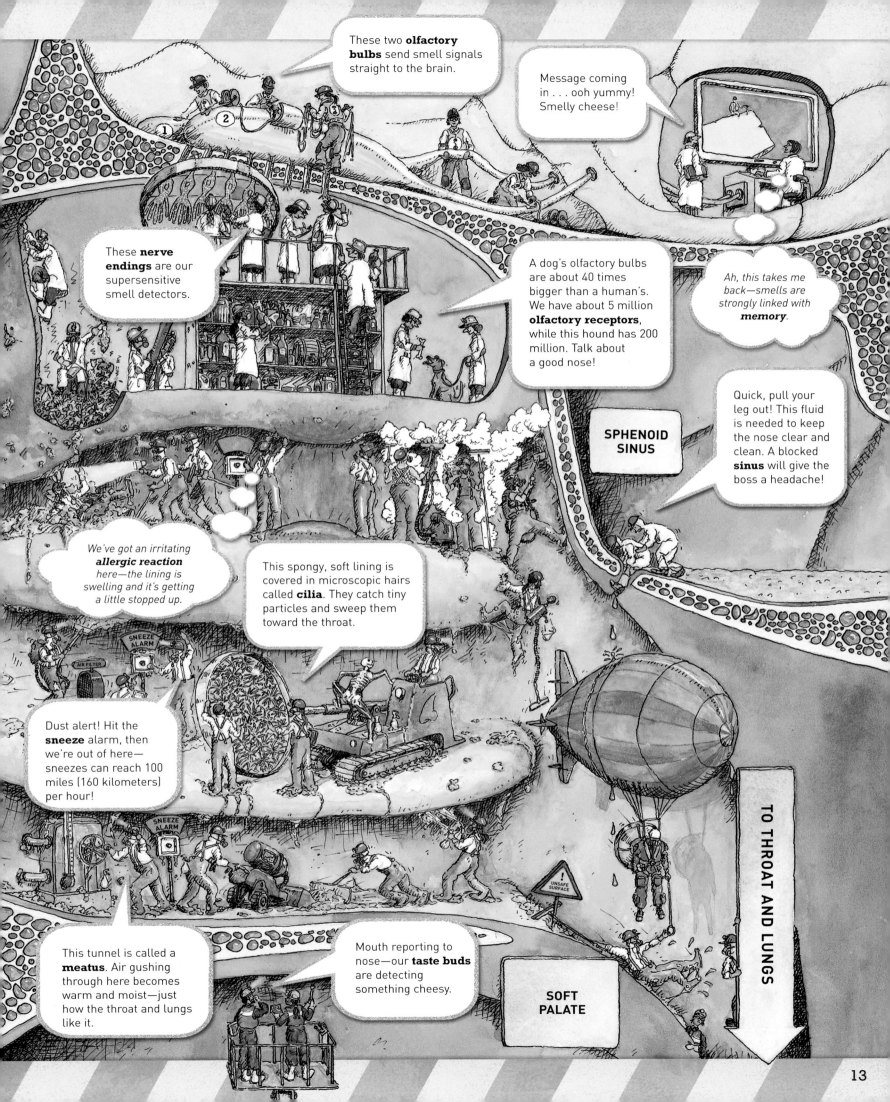

Soaking in slurpy saliva, the mouth is a dangerous work zone. It mashes up almost anything in its path! It is the hatchway for food and drink and the exit hole for coughs, hiccups, and upchucks. This guzzling, grinding, churning, chomping machine is the first stage in your digestive system. Gulp!

YOU ARE HERE

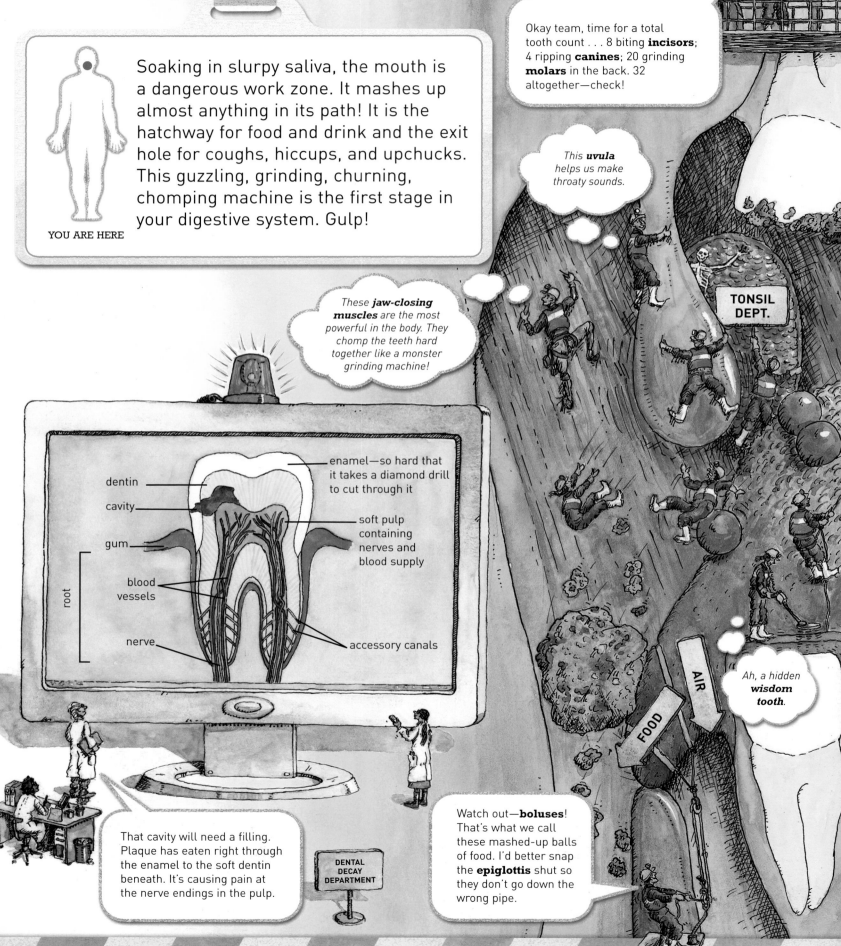

dentin

cavity

gum

blood vessels

root

nerve

enamel—so hard that it takes a diamond drill to cut through it

soft pulp containing nerves and blood supply

accessory canals

Okay team, time for a total tooth count . . . 8 biting **incisors**; 4 ripping **canines**; 20 grinding **molars** in the back. 32 altogether—check!

*This **uvula** helps us make throaty sounds.*

*These **jaw-closing muscles** are the most powerful in the body. They chomp the teeth hard together like a monster grinding machine!*

TONSIL DEPT.

*Ah, a hidden **wisdom tooth**.*

AIR

FOOD

That cavity will need a filling. Plaque has eaten right through the enamel to the soft dentin beneath. It's causing pain at the nerve endings in the pulp.

DENTAL DECAY DEPARTMENT

Watch out—**boluses**! That's what we call these mashed-up balls of food. I'd better snap the **epiglottis** shut so they don't go down the wrong pipe.

These molar **roots** look healthy. Nice pink **gums** with no swelling too—good news!
Well, these gnashers need a good cleaning. Mashed-up food mixed with bacteria makes nasty, acid-producing **plaque**.
DECAY!
DECAY!
Hey, boss, the plaque attack looks bad around here! It's eating away the tooth's **enamel**.
This **taste bud** will send a tasty message to the guys in the brain. But will it be bitter, sweet, salty, sour, or savory?
Stinky breath? Blame these **bacteria**. There are more than 10 billion of them in the mouth—that's more bacteria than people living on Earth!
These bumps are called **papillae**—they contain the taste buds. There are 9,000 of them, all over the tongue. These mushroom-shaped ones give you the strongest taste sensations.
Aaargh, I can't stand it when all **16 tongue muscles** move!
That's right—a good squirt of slimy, spitty **saliva** helps soften food, digest it, and keep the teeth plaque-free.
Can someone from Dental Decay take a look at this, please? I think we've got a **cavity**. Not enough toothbrushing here.
Saliva glands at the ready! We'll squirt some more enzyme-packed liquid magic next time we smell food. In the meantime, say cheese!

Endocrine System

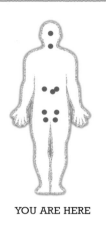

YOU ARE HERE

The hormones of the endocrine system are chemical secret agents, carrying coded messages that change the way body cells operate. Sent out by mysterious glands deep inside the factory, they regulate the balance of substances in the blood and control changes such as growth, becoming adult, and the emotions.

We also send out growth hormones, "love" hormones, and hormones to control how much pee the body makes.

The **pituitary gland** is the "spymaster" of the endocrine system. We send out tons of coded messages, telling other glands to make more or fewer of their hormones.

PITUITARY GLAND

Hurry up, we're on a mission! **Hormones** race round the body in the blood.

Our **thyroid** hormones control how quickly body cells do their jobs and how much **energy** they burn. They also help keep the **heart** and **lungs** working at the right speed.

THYROID GLAND

When the boss exercises or feels stressed, we kick in. Our hormones **cortisol** and **adrenaline** (epinephrine) increase blood sugar levels, rein in the immune system, set the heart racing, and get the body ready for action.

ADRENAL GLAND

I'll take it from here! Every type of hormone has its own **target cells**—the only ones that can crack its code and let it get to work on the body.

I'm a **thyroid-stimulating hormone** with urgent instructions from the pituitary gland. It's time to get those cells working double time!

Woooo, I can feel the **adrenaline** pumping!

HYPOTHALAMUS

*We monitor body temperature and sleep, as well as feelings of hunger, thirst, and tiredness, using signals that come in from the **nervous system**.*

Pineal gland
Hypothalamus
Adrenal glands
Pituitary gland
Thyroid gland
Gonads:
Ovaries (female)
Pancreas
Testes (male)

This poster shows where the main **endocrine glands** are located. Many **organs**, such as the stomach, intestines, kidneys, liver, heart, and lungs, release hormones, too.

PINEAL GLAND

We also spy on the endocrine agents! We run tests on **hormone levels** in the blood and relay all of our data to the pituitary gland.

*Yawn. Our job is to set the Factory's **body clock**. We keep an eye on light levels and tell the boss when it's time to sleep or wake up.*

Men and women have different **gonads**—men have **testes,** and women have **ovaries**. The sex hormones that they produce take charge of the body changes that happen during puberty.

The hormones we make in the **pancreas** control levels of sugary glucose fuel in the blood—**glucagon** increases blood sugar, and **insulin** carries glucose into the body's cells.

PANCREAS

***Blood sugar** needs to be topped off! I'll send some agents to the **liver** with messages to release more glucose from its supplies.*

Mmm, these **hormone levels** are well **balanced**. If there's too much of one kind, the pituitary gland alerts another gland to send out more hormones with the opposite effect.

Skin, Hair, and Nails

Nails protect the ends of the fingers. They lie on a spongy nail bed and grow about 0.1 inches (3 millimeters) per month. They're made from the same material as hair.

Skin is the body's first line of defense. Its tough outer layer is made of old, **dead cells**—and we shed about 30,000 to 40,000 of them every day.

New skin cells form at the bottom of the **epidermis** and gradually move to the surface. My shoveling work is never done!

Every person has a unique set of **fingerprints**. Only this Human Body Factory can make this exact mark!

Luckily for me, the **fingertips** are really **sensitive**. Special cells send messages to the brain so that you know how hard or gently to grip things.

The **dermis** is packed with **sensors** for touch, pain, heat, and cold. Some react to pressure or ticklish vibrations—tee-hee!

YOU ARE HERE

The Human Body Factory is wrapped in a high-tech superskin that keeps it cool, waterproof, and protected from the world outside. The skin is the body's largest organ, covering about 22 square feet (2 square meters) and weighing up to 9 pounds (4 kilograms). It's stuffed full of complex sensors and other gadgets and can repair itself after scrapes and tears.

One of the places that we store fat at the factory is here, under the skin. **Subcutaneous fat** helps keep the body warm, but it's best not to let this layer grow too large!

DERMIS

SUBCUTANEOUS FAT

The skin has three layers—the tough, outer **epidermis**; the stretchy **dermis** beneath it; and then a cushion of spongy **subcutaneous fat**.

More than a trillion **bacteria** live on the skin's surface. They stamp out really nasty germs, but the boss has to wash to stop them from getting out of control.

*Boy, it's hot around here. When the body needs to cool down, more blood flows through **capillaries** near the surface—good news for thirsty mosquitoes!*

*Ah ha, a **mole**! Moles are clusters of the cells that produce **melanin**. Melanin is the stuff that gives your skin its color.*

Whoosh! All this heat has gotten the boss's **sweat** pumping. Sweat comes out through tiny holes in the skin called **pores**. It helps keep the body cool as it evaporates.

EPIDERMIS

OUCH—be careful with that pitchfork! **Nerve endings** warn humans of trouble by sending pain signals back to the brain.

*Sweat is made by sweat **glands** such as this one. Different glands near the surface produce oil, which keeps the skin flexible and waterproof.*

Every **hair** grows from a pit called a **follicle**. It's linked to sensitive **nerve fibers**, as well as a **muscle** that pulls on the hair to give you goose bumps.

Did you know that a thumbnail-size patch of skin contains 50 **nerve endings**, 1,000 touch-sensitive **pressure pads**, 100 **sweat glands** and pores, 1,000 **hairs,** and 100 **oil glands**? Incredible!

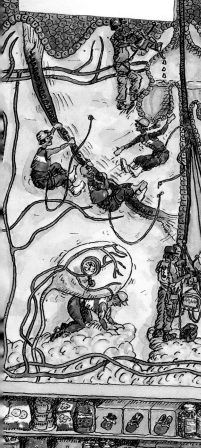

DEPARTMENT: THE ENGINE ROOM
Heart

The beating hub of the Human Body Factory is the heart. This tireless, hard-working department pumps hundreds of gallons of blood around the body every day. It works with the lungs to make sure every body cell gets oxygen. It also helps the blood deliver nutrients and dispose of waste.

YOU ARE HERE

The heart pumps blood in a constant cycle. First, the blood pours into two upper chambers called **atria**. When these are full, they contract, squirting blood down to the lower **ventricles**. Finally, the ventricles contract and squeeze blood out of the heart into the **arteries**.

LUBB-DUPP! The **heartbeat** sound is created as blood passes from atria to ventricles and one set of **valves** closes (lubb). From the ventricles out of the heart a second set closes (dupp).

atria
valves
ventricles

Make way in the **superior vena cava**! This blood has been around the body, delivering oxygen and collecting waste carbon dioxide. It needs to be pumped to the lungs.

TO THE BODY

In the **aorta**, we transport oxygen-rich blood from the lungs toward the rest of the body.

*Okay, okay, I'm going as fast as I can through the **pulmonary artery**! Off to pick up more oxygen from the lungs. . . .*

TO THE LUNGS

Whew, the **pressure** in here's enough to spurt blood across a room!

FROM THE BODY

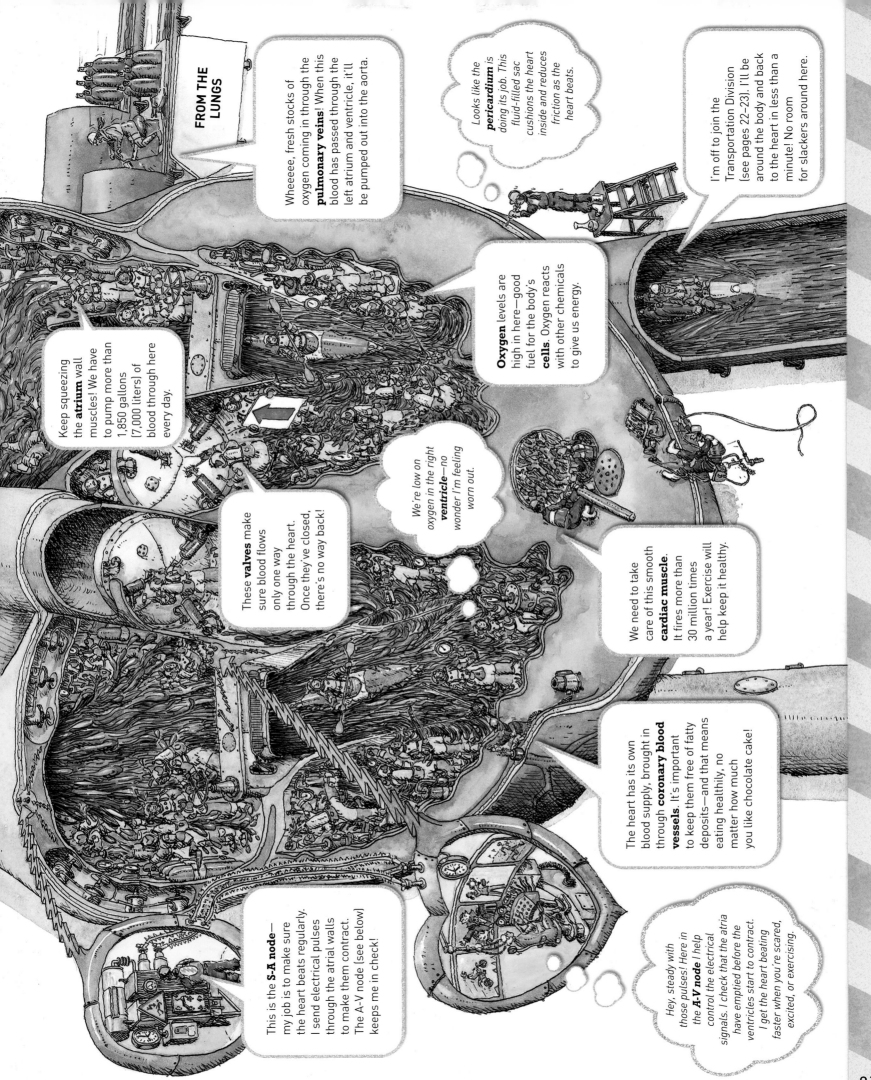

Blood and Circulation

These **artery walls** are really thick and rubbery! They need to be strong to take the pressure of the rushing blood.

Pressure is high here because the blood is shooting straight from the pumping heart.

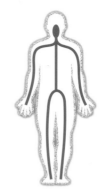

YOU ARE HERE

The factory would quickly grind to a halt without its Transportation Division—the blood. This fast-moving stuff delivers vital oxygen, fuel, and nutrients to the body's cells and removes their waste. It travels through tunnels called blood vessels and is pumped by the engine room—the heart.

FROM THE HEART

Blood whizzes round the body in a strict one-way system—**arteries** travel from the heart, and **veins** go back toward it. The round trip is called **circulation**.

I detect a **pulse**—the throbbing from the heart pumping blood. It beats about 60–80 times a minute when the boss is resting.

plasma
white blood cells
red blood cells

Red blood cells contain an iron-rich chemical called **hemoglobin**. This chemical picks up oxygen in the lungs, turning the blood bright red.

The liquid part of blood is called **plasma**. It's mostly salty water and is pale yellow in color. Blood cells float in it, while other stuff is dissolved in it.

Blood pressure is the force with which the heart pumps blood through the blood vessels. It can rise during exercise, when your heart works harder.

The boss needs to cut down on fatty foods! They can cause excess **cholesterol**, which gunks up smaller arteries and blocks the blood supply to body cells.

Veins have thinner walls than arteries do because the pressure inside them is lower. Muscles pump the blood along, and **valves** stop it from sloshing backward.

artery

vein

Blood vessels reach every part of the body. The biggest (the aorta) is 1 inch (2.5 centimeters) wide and 16 inches (40 centimeters) long. As the tubes branch out, they get smaller—capillaries are barely the width of one red blood cell.

TO THE HEART

The tiniest blood vessels, called **capillaries**, have teeny gaps in their walls. Oxygen and nutrients slip through into the body cells, while waste goes the other way.

An adult Human Body Factory has about **10.5 pints (5 liters) of blood**. We can lose a third of it and survive, but losing half may be fatal!

CO_2

Quick—send in the **platelets** to patch over this cut! These special cells stem the flow of blood and plug the hole with a thick seal.

SUPPLIES
to body cells

In the veins we carry cell waste such as **carbon dioxide, urea,** and **lactic acid**. There's less oxygen here than in the arteries, so the blood is darker red.

CO_2

WASTE
from body cells

Hormones like me are dissolved in the blood. We carry coded messages that affect growth, moods, and the rate that cells work.

White blood cells come from the immune system. We're here to destroy bacteria, viruses, and other bad guys.

In just one drop of healthy blood there are about **5 million red blood cells, 8,000 white blood cells,** and **300,000 platelets**. Wow!

BLOOD CELL CHECKPOINT

RED CELLS

WHITE CELLS

PLATELETS

Immune System

YOU ARE HERE

The Emergency Response Team is the body's protection force, defending it against disease. The cells of the immune system tirelessly patrol the blood and lymphatic channels, hunting for invading microbes. You don't mess with these guys! When they find viruses and bacteria, they blast them with specialized and lethal weapons.

Working with **lymph** is a squelchy business! This clear, syrupy fluid surrounds the body's cells. It carries away waste that the fast-moving blood can't pick up.

White blood cells are designed to fight infection and destroy disease. They can pass from the blood to body cells through gaps in capillary walls. They patrol the lymph fluid, too.

Lymph dribbles and seeps along its own pipes called **lymph capillaries**.

Easily dissolvable waste such as carbon dioxide goes straight back into the bloodstream, but lymph takes fragments of **damaged cells** and **microbes** with it.

LYMPH NODE

Lymph drains into 500–600 **lymph nodes** like this, where we clean it. We also gather immune cells and teach them how to recognize invaders.

We filter the lymph to remove **dead cells**, **damaged tissues,** and other junk. Then we screen it for nasty microorganisms.

*Infections have a tough time getting past our security check! After screening for invaders, we add chemical agents called **antibodies** to the lymph, and then send this juice into the lymphatic system.*

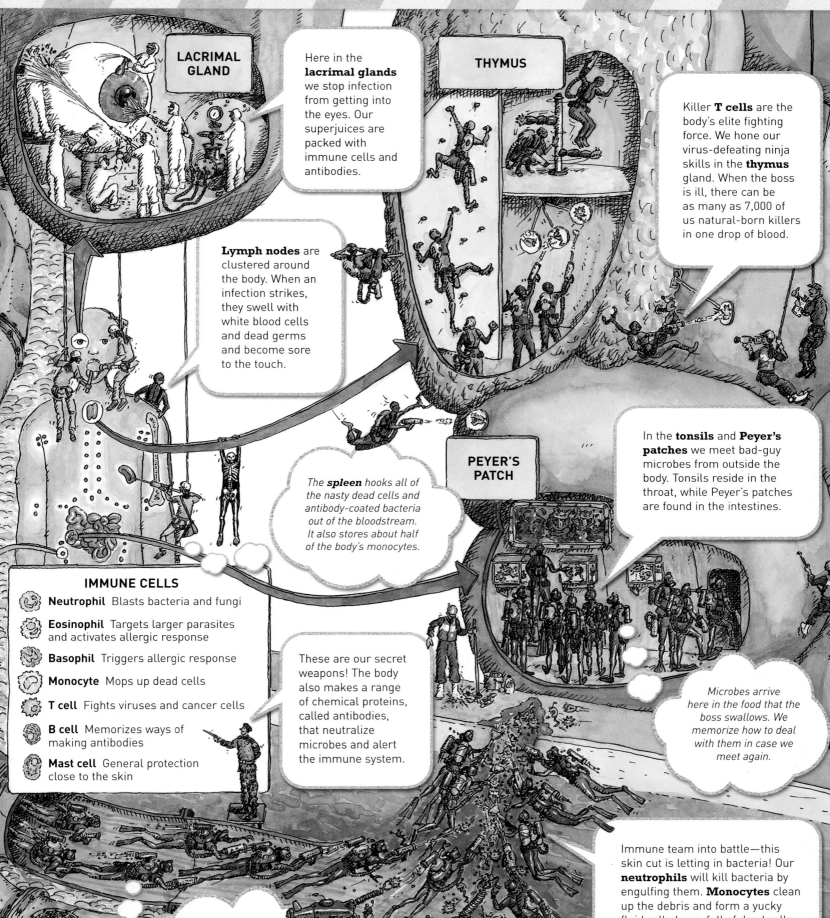

LACRIMAL GLAND

Here in the **lacrimal glands** we stop infection from getting into the eyes. Our superjuices are packed with immune cells and antibodies.

THYMUS

Killer **T cells** are the body's elite fighting force. We hone our virus-defeating ninja skills in the **thymus** gland. When the boss is ill, there can be as many as 7,000 of us natural-born killers in one drop of blood.

Lymph nodes are clustered around the body. When an infection strikes, they swell with white blood cells and dead germs and become sore to the touch.

The **spleen** hooks all of the nasty dead cells and antibody-coated bacteria out of the bloodstream. It also stores about half of the body's monocytes.

PEYER'S PATCH

In the **tonsils** and **Peyer's patches** we meet bad-guy microbes from outside the body. Tonsils reside in the throat, while Peyer's patches are found in the intestines.

IMMUNE CELLS

Neutrophil Blasts bacteria and fungi

Eosinophil Targets larger parasites and activates allergic response

Basophil Triggers allergic response

Monocyte Mops up dead cells

T cell Fights viruses and cancer cells

B cell Memorizes ways of making antibodies

Mast cell General protection close to the skin

These are our secret weapons! The body also makes a range of chemical proteins, called antibodies, that neutralize microbes and alert the immune system.

Microbes arrive here in the food that the boss swallows. We memorize how to deal with them in case we meet again.

Immune team into battle—this skin cut is letting in bacteria! Our **neutrophils** will kill bacteria by engulfing them. **Monocytes** clean up the debris and form a yucky fluid called pus, full of dead cells.

B cells like us rove the blood looking out for microbes we've met before. We remember how to defeat them and get the body to start brewing antibodies.

25

Bones and Joints

YOU ARE HERE

The Human Body Factory is built around a tough inner framework—the skeleton. This bundle of bones supports the body's weight, protects vital organs, and provides anchor points for muscles to pull on. Where bones meet at joints, a complex system of pulleys and cords allows the body to flex and bend. It's important to take care of this department—after all, without it you'd be a floppy heap!

JOINT SHOP

Hinge	Pivot	Ball and socket	Gliding	Saddle
knee	neck	shoulder	backbone	thumb
elbow	forearm	hip	ankle, wrist	

This jellylike stuff inside the bone is **bone marrow**. Its job is to make your blood cells—including 175 billion fresh red blood cells every day. Surrounding the marrow is a soft but strong honeycomb of **spongy bone**.

Wow, 206 bones in an adult skeleton!

Get your **joints** here! Wherever two bones meet, you need the right joint to let them move properly. There are also some fixed joints, such as the ones in your skull.

The hard outer layer is called **compact bone**. It's packed with living **osteocyte** cells that have their own blood supply. Bones may seem like dead things, but in fact they're very much alive!

The knee is the body's largest joint—and one of the hardest working. Between the bones is a pocket of **synovial fluid**, which oils the joint to keep it moving smoothly.

*Bone food on its way! **Calcium** helps keep bones hard and strong—we get it from dairy products and even some vegetables, fruits, and nuts. Vitamin D from sunlight is good for bones, too.*

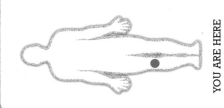

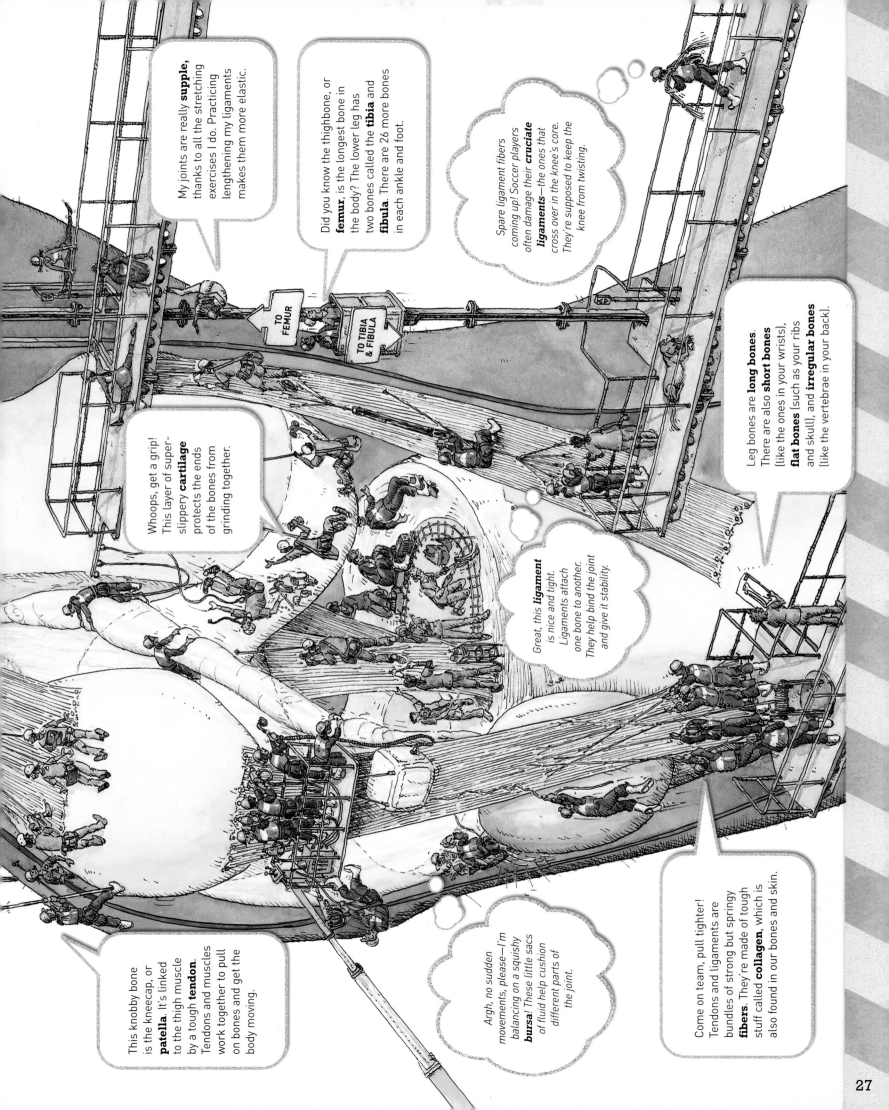

Muscles

Muscles work in pairs to pull on bones. To lift the lower arm, the **biceps** here **contracts**, or tightens up.

Come on, blood team, keep the **oxygen**, **water,** and **glucose** coming! The muscles need these to make and burn their fuel, called **ATP**. Without it, the boss would get weak!

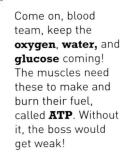

BLOOD SUPPLIES

WATER

GLUCOSE

While the biceps contracts, the **triceps** underneath the arm **relaxes** and lengthens out.

Muscles are made up of lots of stringy **fibers**. *Only one-third of all fibers contract at the same time when the muscle is working at full power.*

LACTIC ACID DISPOSAL

All of this muscle action **burns energy** *and warms the body. I'm taking a break, but not for long! To lower the arm, it's the triceps that does the work.*

RELAX

Uh-oh—I'm reading a buildup of **lactic acid** waste. If we don't get oxygen into the muscle fast, I'm afraid the boss will get a **cramp**.

Electrical impulses from tiny **nerve fibers** trigger each strand of muscle to contract. Skeletal muscles such as the biceps are controlled by the boss's brain.

Your body has about **320 muscle pairs,** and they make up more than half of your weight. Exercising them can make you strong like me!

Show-off! Bet you don't know that **blood flow** *to the muscles increases by up to 12 times during exercise.*

When it's time to get moving, the muscly machinists of the Motion Unit set to work. They operate the muscles that shift the body around, move it from place to place, and help it stay fit. But that's not all that the muscles do. They also drive internal organs, coordinate the heartbeat, and control the fine movements of the eyes. So come on, lazybones—action, please!

YOU ARE HERE

MUSCLE YARD

Get your pecs here!

A skeletal   **B** cardiac   **C** smooth

A

B

C

There are three types of muscles up for grabs here. High-powered **skeletal muscle** moves bones around; tireless **cardiac muscle** keeps the heart beating nonstop; and slick **smooth muscle** helps control many other internal organs.

What we have here is a **fascicle**—it's a single muscle cable built with bunches of connected muscle fibers.

Nothing happens inside muscle cells without **calcium**. Milk truck to the rescue—fresh supplies coming up!

If we looked even closer, we'd see a network of tiny blood vessels called **capillaries**. They bring a constant supply of nutrients and oxygen to the muscle cells.

Muscles are attached to bones by tough cords called **tendons**. They help the biceps and triceps pull on the lower arm like a lever.

The muscle cells in these "smart fibers" can be as long as a 12-inch (30-centimeter) ruler! They're made up of **microscopic filaments** that lie end to end when the muscle is **relaxed**.

When a muscle fiber **contracts**, the microscopic filaments slide over one another like interlacing fingers. This action shortens the fiber, pulling the ends of the muscle together and making it bulge.

29

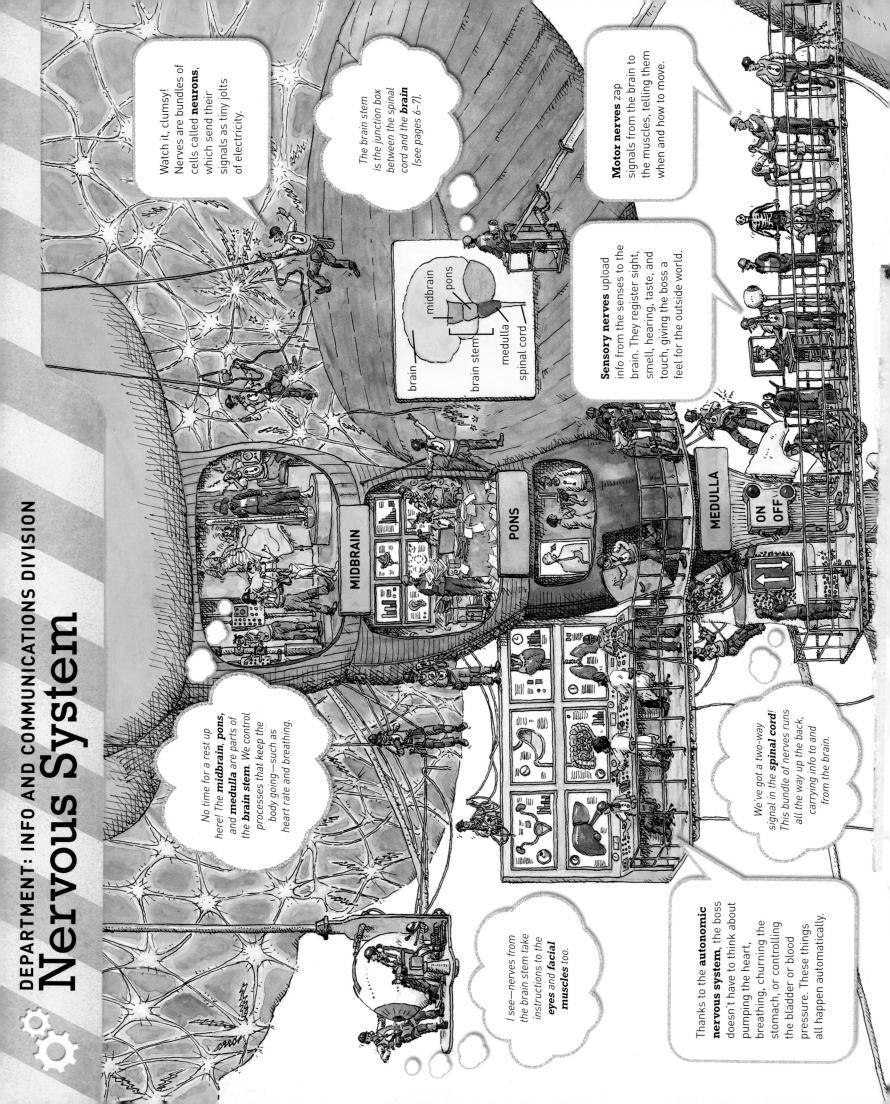

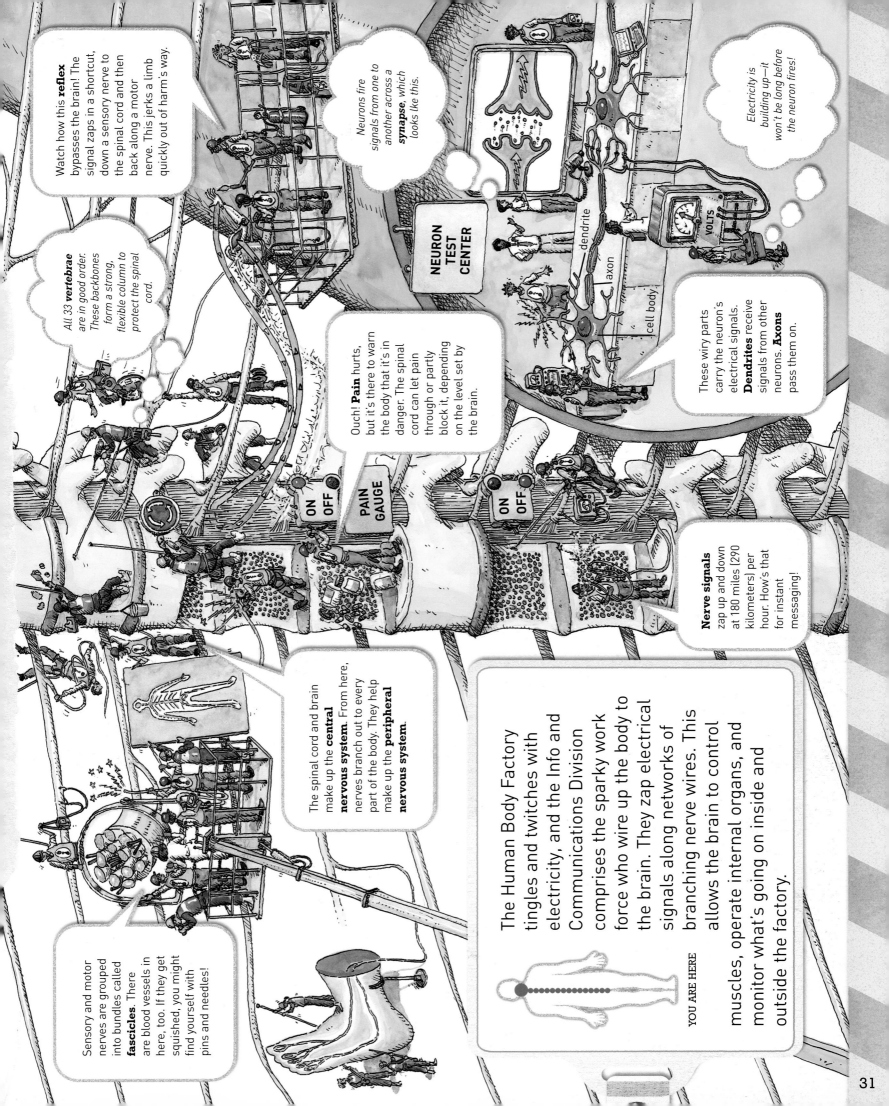

Watch how this **reflex** bypasses the brain! The signal zaps in a shortcut, down a sensory nerve to the spinal cord and then back along a motor nerve. This jerks a limb quickly out of harm's way.

Neurons fire signals from one to another across a **synapse,** *which looks like this.*

Electricity is building up—it won't be long before the neuron fires!

All 33 **vertebrae** *are in good order. These backbones form a strong, flexible column to protect the spinal cord.*

NEURON TEST CENTER

VOLTS

dendrite

axon

cell body

These wiry parts carry the neuron's electrical signals. **Dendrites** receive signals from other neurons. **Axons** pass them on.

Ouch! **Pain** hurts, but it's there to warn the body that it's in danger. The spinal cord can let pain through or partly block it, depending on the level set by the brain.

ON OFF

PAIN GAUGE

ON OFF

Nerve signals zap up and down at 180 miles (290 kilometers) per hour. How's that for instant messaging!

Sensory and motor nerves are grouped into bundles called **fascicles.** There are blood vessels in here, too. If they get squished, you might find yourself with pins and needles!

The spinal cord and brain make up the **central nervous system.** From here, nerves branch out to every part of the body. They help make up the **peripheral nervous system.**

The Human Body Factory tingles and twitches with electricity, and the Info and Communications Division comprises the sparky work force who wire up the body to the brain. They zap electrical signals along networks of branching nerve wires. This allows the brain to control muscles, operate internal organs, and monitor what's going on inside and outside the factory.

YOU ARE HERE

31

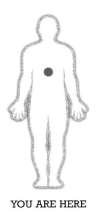

YOU ARE HERE

The lungs are where Human Body Factory workers go to stay fit. Their job is to get vital oxygen into the body and force poisonous carbon dioxide out. Air enters and leaves the lungs through a maze of branching tubes that end in tiny gas exchange pods. You need a lot of puff to work in this department. Take a deep breath!

We're here to keep the **intercostal muscles** working. They have to lift and lower the **rib cage** every time we breathe— that's around 20,000 times a day!

Okay team, check the **cartilage** rings that keep these big air pipes open. There are 1,500 miles (2,400 kilometers) of tubes in here. The tiniest ones are called **bronchioles**.

When you **breathe in**, your diaphragm (beneath the lungs) pulls downward. At the same time, intercostal muscles (in your chest) lift your ribs up and outward. This creates space for air to rush into your lungs. They inflate just like balloons!

You **breathe out** when your diaphragm and intercostal muscles relax. The diaphragm springs upward, the ribs close in, and air whistles out of your lungs to leave through your nose or mouth.

Good, a thin layer of fluid lining the **pleura**. This covering cushions and protects the lungs as you breathe.

Keep pulling down on the **diaphragm**! This sheet of muscle is like a set of industrial bellows, forcing air in and out of the lungs.

Great, the **vocal cords** are nice and tight. They vibrate to make sounds when we speak.

Did you know the **surface area** inside the lungs is as big as a tennis court?

Amazing! That's because each tiny tube ends in air sacs called **alveoli**. A pair of lungs has 600 million of them! The alveoli are stretchy—as they fill with air, the lungs get bigger.

Wheee! It's windy in this windpipe, or **trachea**. One pint (0.5 liters) of air comes in with every breath!

The alveoli are where **gas exchange** takes place. Each air sac is covered in a mesh of fine **capillaries**. These, and the alveoli, have really thin walls that let oxygen pass into the blood while carbon dioxide passes out.

Here in the **bronchi**, slimy mucus and microscopic hairs help clear out any dust that's breathed in.

Wow, and all of this happens without us even thinking about it!

No jerky movements, please! An irritated diaphragm causes **hiccups**. Hic!

We really have to work hard when the boss goes running! When you **exercise**, your body cells need more oxygen, so you breathe deeper and faster to bring in extra air.

Liver and Gall Bladder

EXIT (HEPATIC VEIN)

We're in charge of **breaking down toxins**. Once they've been neutralized, we chuck some out with the bile. The rest go in the blood to the kidneys, to be filtered out of the body.

The liver is a wizard at sorting good things from bad. **Poisons** get whisked away, while **medicines** are broken down and activated so they can get to work in the body.

WASTE

Be careful with these blood barrels! As well as goodies like **vitamins**, **sugars**, **iron,** and **fats**, there are some nasty **toxins** that slip in through the mouth portal.

The liver's main jobs are done by chemical-reaction units called **enzymes**. Meanwhile, **immune cells** roam around to destroy microbes and clean up.

It's bustling here in the body's **largest internal organ**. We manage 500 separate tasks—dicing, slicing, grinding, and grating up ingredients carried in the blood.

DELIVERIES

We replace damaged **liver cells** every year or so—this trooper will still do its work with many of them out of action. Even so, it's better to steer clear of harmful stuff if you love your liver!

FULL UP

HUNGRY

Bile is a bitter green liquid, made to dissolve fats in the intestines. The liver produces 2 pints (1 liter) of bile every day and the **gall bladder** stores it. Glub!

I have to wait for the **stomach** to release its contents into the **intestines**. Then I scrunch the gall bladder and squirt bile down the tubes to help **digest** the food.

When the level of **nitrogen** in the blood rises, we convert it into **urea**, which leaves the body in the boss's pee. Urea breaks down into stinky ammonia, which is why pee can smell!

Many **vitamins** from food make their way here in the blood. We store them for when the body needs them.

We concoct **vitamin A** from the carotene in carrots—it's great for healthy skin and eyesight. We also help activate **vitamin D**, for strong bones and teeth.

Iron is a mineral found in foods such as red meat and leafy vegetables. It's vital for building **new red blood cells**, so we grind up any spare scraps and store them.

I've got a load of waste from the **spleen**, made from **old red blood cells**. We juice it up so the liver and kidneys can get rid of it. It's what makes pee yellow.

I'm making **glycogen** energy bars from the **carbohydrates** in starchy foods. They can be stored by the body for a long time.

UREA

BILE

When the boss needs an energy boost, we convert glycogen to **glucose**. A hormone called **insulin**, made in the pancreas, regulates the amount of energy available for the body to use.

We work at night, making **cholesterol**. This substance goes into the bile and passes into the blood by way of the small intestine. It's used to build cell walls and make hormones.

Chop-chop, chefs! Menu of the day is gloppy **bile** soup and a dash of thin **blood-plasma protein** sauce.

HEPATIC PORTAL VEIN

HEPATIC ARTERY

YOU ARE HERE

Right in the middle of the Human Body Factory is a wedge-shaped, workaholic organ—the liver. Like a huge, hectic kitchen, it processes raw ingredients brought in by blood from the stomach and intestines. The liver whips up bile, refines and stores sugar and nutrients, and cleans the blood. It's hot work, and the heat pumped out by all of this action warms the whole body.

Coming in—a delivery of **blood** from the stomach and intestines! The **hepatic portal vein** is the only vein in the body that doesn't flow directly toward the heart.

Kidneys and Bladder

The kidneys are a pair of steamy, gushy treatment plants where toxic waste and excess water are removed from the blood. These complex, high-pressure filtering units clean 460 gallons (1,750 liters) of blood every day. They also produce about 3 pints (1.5 liters) of urine, which flows to a bag called the bladder before exiting the body for good.

YOU ARE HERE

*Wow, there are 40 miles (65 kilometers) of nephrons in the kidney. No wonder the blood comes out clean! I'm taking it down the **renal vein** back to the rest of the body.*

BODY FLUID LOSS

URINE 55%

water vapor from lungs

evaporation from skin

solid waste

sweat

The body is about two-thirds water, but we need to keep the balance right. We get rid of excess water in various ways. As you can see, the main one is **urination** (peeing).

Shipment of dirty blood coming in! Blood in the **renal artery** contains waste from the body and needs to be cleaned.

DIRTY BLOOD

CLEAN BLOOD

TO BLADDER

ADRENAL GLAND

In this section we remove any useful **sugars, salts, minerals,** and **proteins** from the urine and put them back into the blood.

Whew, I'm tired. Here in the **kidneys** we filter the body's blood at least 300 times a day. We also help balance the volume of fluids and salts in the body.

*The watery parts of the blood, along with waste chemicals and some important nutrients, get squeezed out under **high pressure.** They are turned into a clear, yellowish liquid called **urine.***

Each filtering unit is called a **nephron.** There are around a million of them in each kidney—and they're tiny. Here's a close-up look at one.

The high-pressure filter works a little like a coffee machine. Pssssssst.

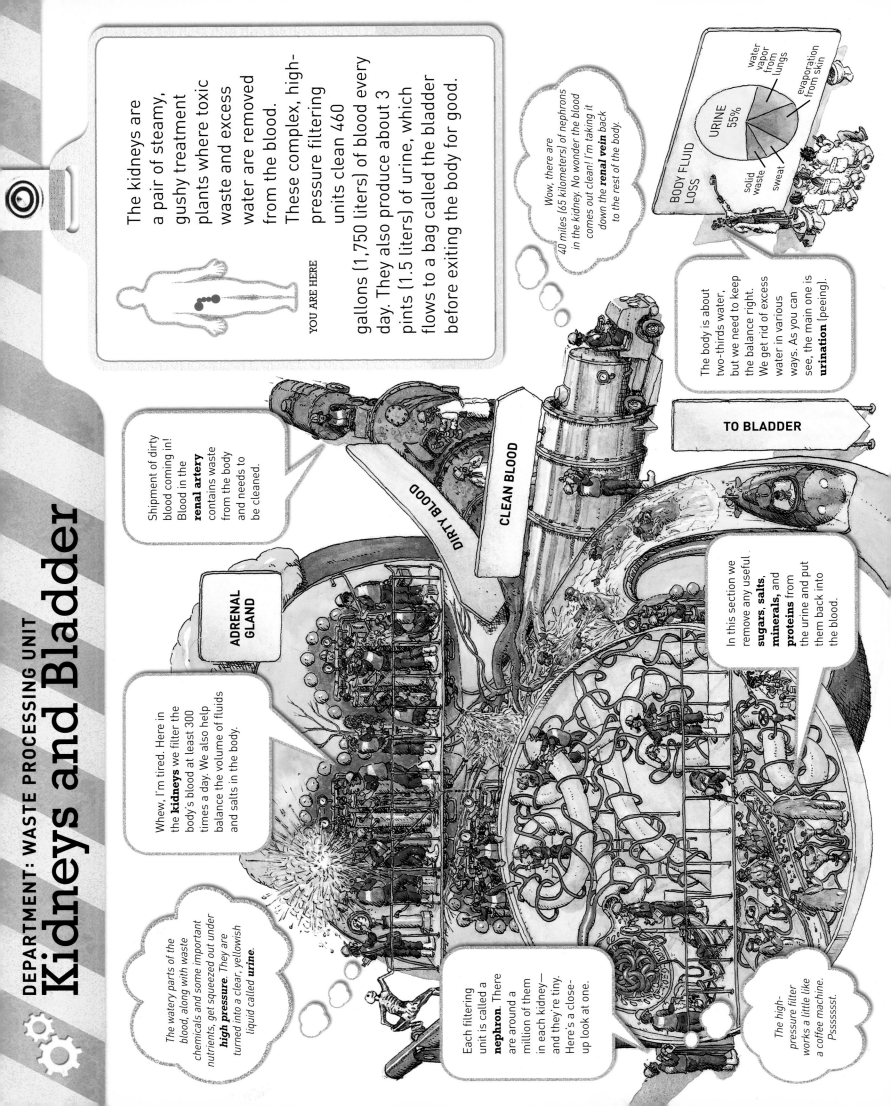

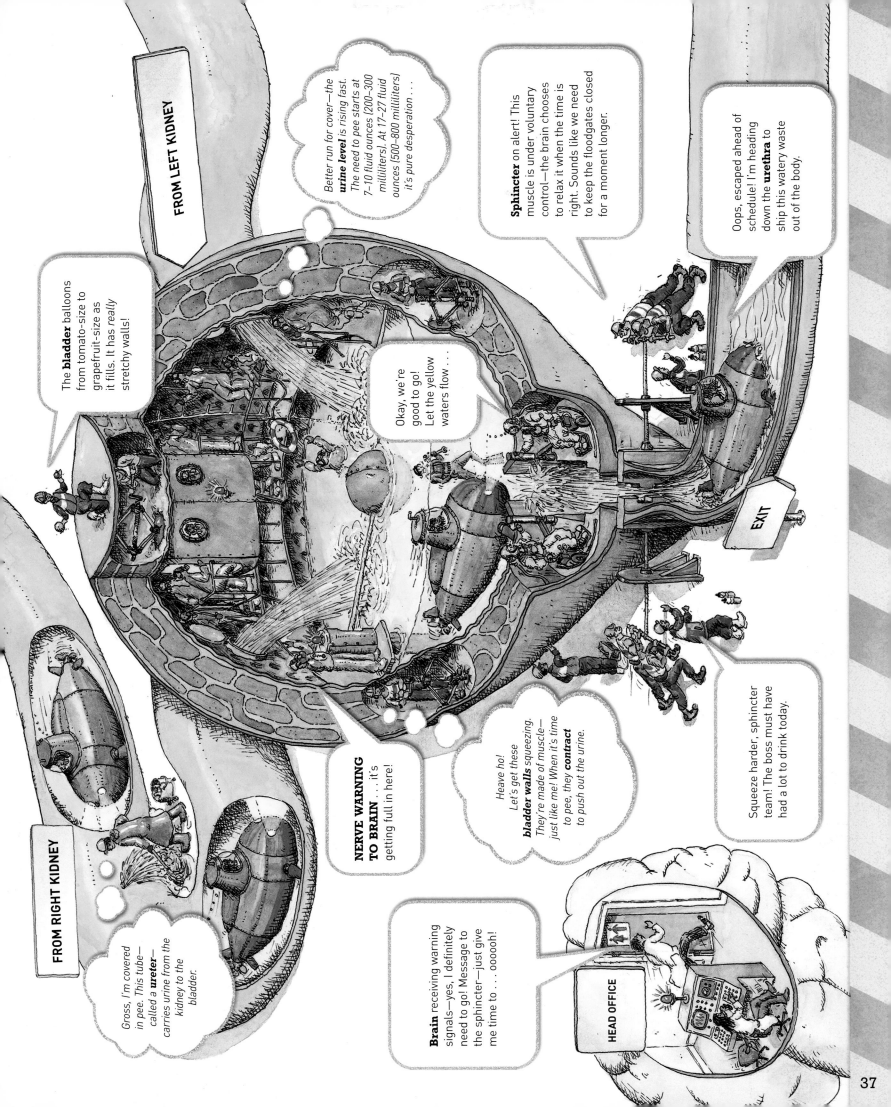

Digestion

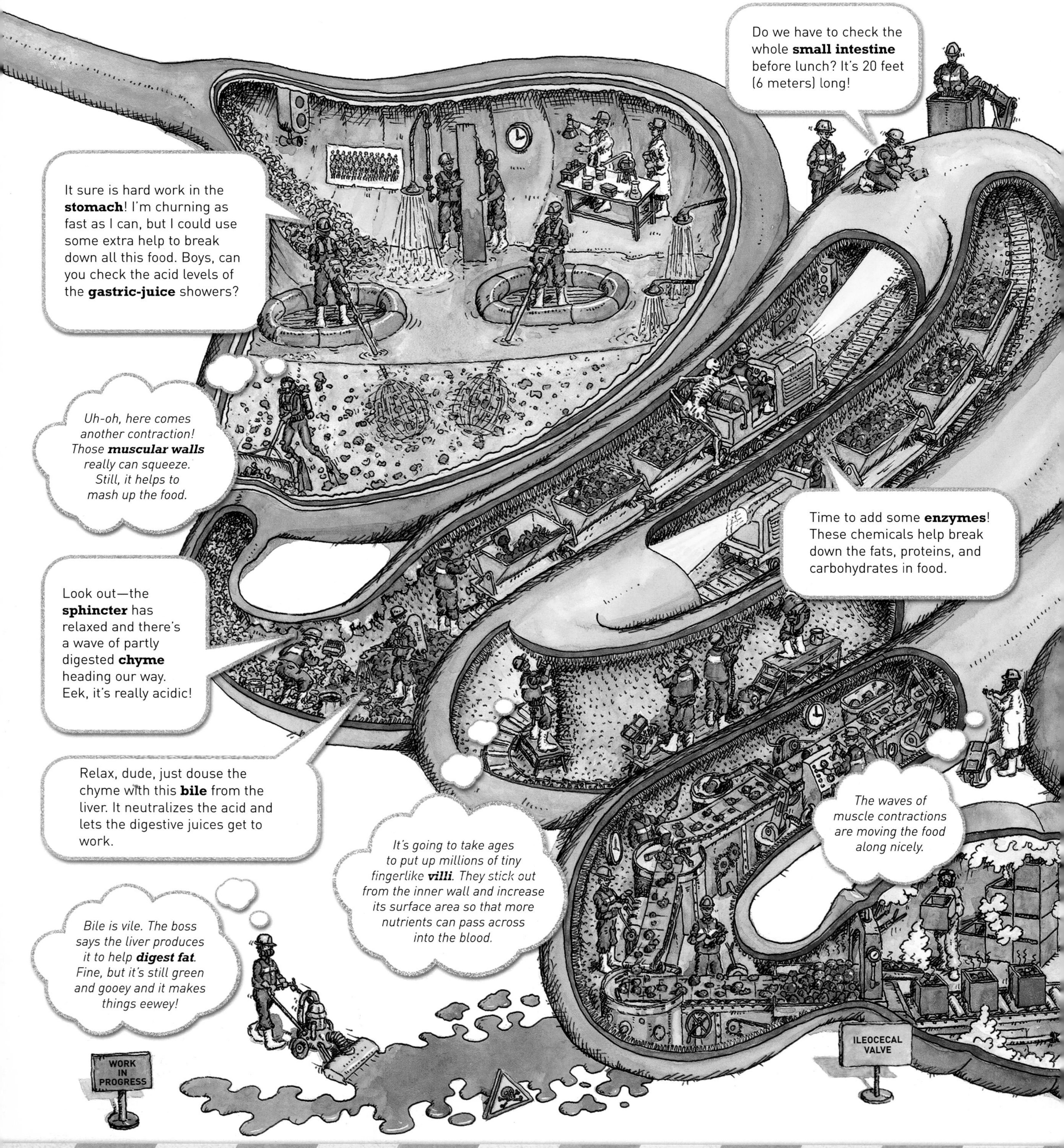

Do we have to check the whole **small intestine** before lunch? It's 20 feet (6 meters) long!

It sure is hard work in the **stomach**! I'm churning as fast as I can, but I could use some extra help to break down all this food. Boys, can you check the acid levels of the **gastric-juice** showers?

Uh-oh, here comes another contraction! Those **muscular walls** really can squeeze. Still, it helps to mash up the food.

Time to add some **enzymes**! These chemicals help break down the fats, proteins, and carbohydrates in food.

Look out—the **sphincter** has relaxed and there's a wave of partly digested **chyme** heading our way. Eek, it's really acidic!

Relax, dude, just douse the chyme with this **bile** from the liver. It neutralizes the acid and lets the digestive juices get to work.

It's going to take ages to put up millions of tiny fingerlike **villi**. They stick out from the inner wall and increase its surface area so that more nutrients can pass across into the blood.

The waves of muscle contractions are moving the food along nicely.

Bile is vile. The boss says the liver produces it to help **digest fat**. Fine, but it's still green and gooey and it makes things eewey!

WORK IN PROGRESS

ILEOCECAL VALVE

Keep an eye on the clock, everyone. Remember—the food should take no more than 48 hours from the stomach to ejection.

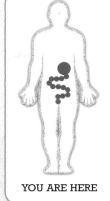
YOU ARE HERE

The body needs food for energy and to make repairs, but what goes in must come out! Once the nutrients have been absorbed into the bloodstream, there are waste products to deal with. Over to the workers in the digestion department—they have one of the stinkiest jobs in the body.

Watch out—it's slippery in the **rectum**! We need all that **mucus** to help the waste slide out.

Okay, let's get this waste packed up and ready to go. We've got about 12 hours to get it through the **large intestine**.

Turn on that vacuum cleaner. We need to suck out most of the water. I'll squirt out trillions of "**friendly**" **bacteria** to eat any undigested waste.

Thank goodness for gas masks—the boss has been eating too many baked beans!

With a gusty burst of **flatulence**, we've made it out of the **anus**! Mission accomplished!

Reproduction

Here in the **seminal vesicles** we brew up a sugar-filled energy drink to give sperm swimmers extra power.

Okay team, clear the tubes! The Waste Processing Unit is on alert, and we're about to empty the **bladder**.

YOU ARE HERE

The New Model Planning Unit has a unique job—instead of keeping the body alive, it works for the future! Males and females have different reproductive parts, but both produce an unusual type of cell with only a half-portion of genes (the instructions for human life). When a male sperm and a female egg meet and their genes mix, they make a brand-new person.

The dangly part below is the **penis**. I can make it stiffen by pumping in extra blood.

In the **prostate gland** we produce a milky liquid. Our muscle pumps can squirt it through the penis to help sperm on their way.

Lift or drop? This sack, called the **scrotum**, holds the **testes**. When they're cold, I pull them up so the body can warm them. When they're hot, I lower them down to cool off.

This tube, called the **urethra**, transports pee as well as sperm out of the penis. We need to keep all of these parts clean and bacteria-free.

An adult man's testes are busy **sperm** factories. We churn out these wrigglers nonstop! Each sperm is just 0.02 inches (0.05 millimeters) long.

We train sperm so they can **swim** when they enter a woman's body. Their aim is to reach and **fertilize** an **egg**.

Millions of sperm are stored inside the twisty **epididymis**. When it's time for them to leave the body, they move up into the **vas deferens** tube.

It's my job to make **testosterone**. This hormone drives the changes that happen during **puberty**, such as growing more body hair.

MAN

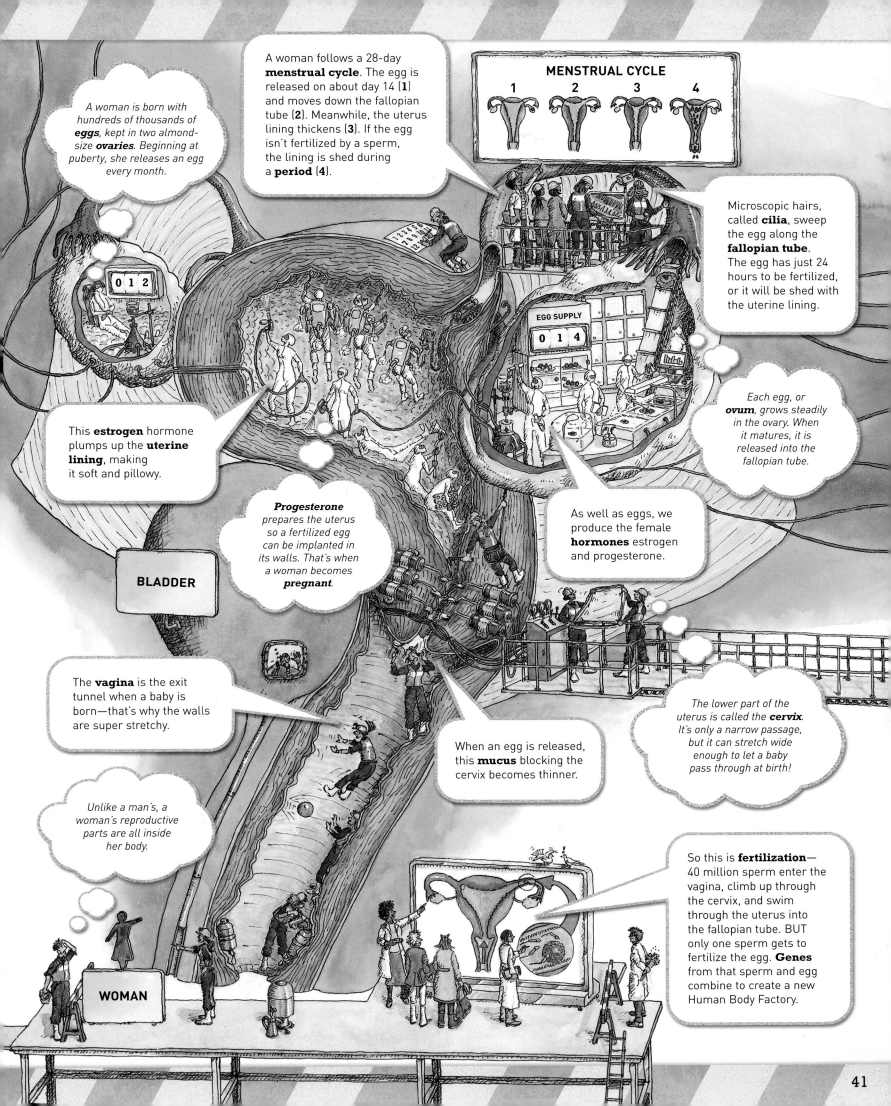

Pregnancy

UTERUS

*We need more **progesterone** to plump up this lining.*

Woo hoo! We've got a **fertilization**! Millions of sperm may reach the egg, but only one winner gets through its outer wall.

FROM OVARY

DAY 1

DAY 3

DAY 4

The sperm and egg fuse to form a single **cell**. In 24 hours this cell divides in two. It keeps dividing, and after about three days it's a ball of lots of cells.

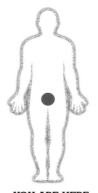

YOU ARE HERE

Making a teeny-weeny new model is one of the most amazing things a Human Body Factory can do. The female body contains all of the equipment needed to grow a new unit, but first one of her eggs must join with a male's sperm. It takes about 40 weeks of pregnancy to develop the new model to the stage at which it can survive in the outside world.

Ready for **implantation**! The ball of cells now settles into the **uterine wall**. Parts of it develop separately to form the yolk sac, placenta and amnion.

*We don't need this **yolk sac** now that the embryo is getting food from its mom.*

Good, the **amnion** is strong! This fluid-filled bag protects the developing baby from bumps.

The **placenta** lets oxygen and nutrients pass from the mom's blood to the developing baby's. Waste goes in the other direction—but the two blood supplies never mix. The **umbilical cord** connects the developing baby to the placenta.

placenta

umbilical cord

mother's blood—nutrients

baby's blood

waste

*There's not much thinking going on yet, but the **brain** is definitely starting to take shape!*

At this stage, the developing baby is called an **embryo**. It's only the size of a pea.

6 WEEKS

*It doesn't look very human yet—the limbs are just buds, the **hands** and **feet** are webbed, and it has a **tail**!*

Excellent, the **heart** is just coming online—we have a pulse!

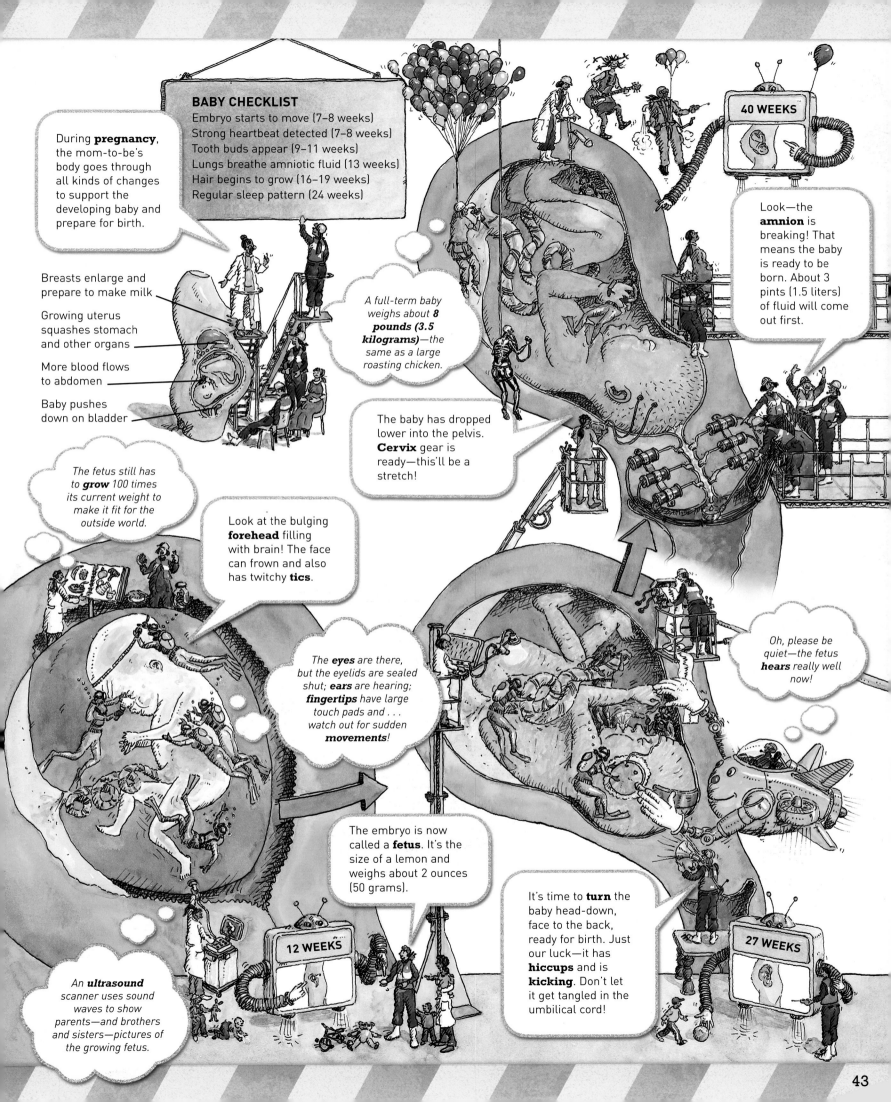

BABY CHECKLIST
Embryo starts to move (7–8 weeks)
Strong heartbeat detected (7–8 weeks)
Tooth buds appear (9–11 weeks)
Lungs breathe amniotic fluid (13 weeks)
Hair begins to grow (16–19 weeks)
Regular sleep pattern (24 weeks)

During **pregnancy**, the mom-to-be's body goes through all kinds of changes to support the developing baby and prepare for birth.

Breasts enlarge and prepare to make milk

Growing uterus squashes stomach and other organs

More blood flows to abdomen

Baby pushes down on bladder

A full-term baby weighs about **8 pounds (3.5 kilograms)**—the same as a large roasting chicken.

The fetus still has to **grow** 100 times its current weight to make it fit for the outside world.

Look at the bulging **forehead** filling with brain! The face can frown and also has twitchy **tics**.

The baby has dropped lower into the pelvis. **Cervix** gear is ready—this'll be a stretch!

40 WEEKS

Look—the **amnion** is breaking! That means the baby is ready to be born. About 3 pints (1.5 liters) of fluid will come out first.

The **eyes** are there, but the eyelids are sealed shut; **ears** are hearing; **fingertips** have large touch pads and . . . watch out for sudden **movements**!

Oh, please be quiet—the fetus **hears** really well now!

The embryo is now called a **fetus**. It's the size of a lemon and weighs about 2 ounces (50 grams).

12 WEEKS

An **ultrasound** scanner uses sound waves to show parents—and brothers and sisters—pictures of the growing fetus.

It's time to **turn** the baby head-down, face to the back, ready for birth. Just our luck—it has **hiccups** and is **kicking**. Don't let it get tangled in the umbilical cord!

27 WEEKS

Amazing Body Facts

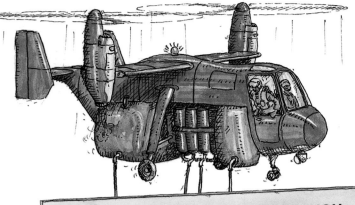

From the moment you leave your mother's womb, pop out into the world, and take your first breath, your body is working hard to keep you up and running. It does a million marvelous things for you—like reading this book, for instance! Life is full of mind-boggling surprises . . .

THE HUMAN BODY CONTAINS ENOUGH . . .

Carbon to make about 900 pencils
Nitrogen to fill a soda can
Phosphorus to make 2,000 matches
Iron for a standard nail
Sulfur to de-flea a dog
Fat to make seven bars of soap
Water to fill ten gallon-size milk jugs!

BODY FACT FILE

Number of bones: 206*

Average body temperature: 98.6 °F (37 °C)

Average pulse rate: 60–90 beats per minute; athletes as low as 40 bpm*

Average total blood volume: 10.5 pints (5 liters)*

Average brain weight: 3 lb. (1.4kg)*

Number of brain cells: more than 10 billion

Number of brain cells lost every day: 85,000

Total dead skin shed in a lifetime: approx. 40 lb. (18kg)

Number of cell types: approx. 220

Number of muscles: approx. 650

Total surface area of skin: approx. 20 sq. ft. (1.86m²)*

Total surface area of alveoli (in lungs): approx. 750 sq. ft. (70m²)*

* These facts refer to an adult Human Body Factory (the others refer to all body factories)

The ridges on your fingers can feel minuscule bumps 0.00004 inches (0.001 millimeters) across—about a hundred times smaller than anything you can see with your eyes!

Glossary

Abdomen The middle part of the body, below the ribs, that contains the stomach, intestines, liver, kidneys, and several other organs.

Adrenal gland An organ that sits on top of each kidney and responds to stress by making hormones such as epinephrine (adrenaline) and cortisol.

Antibodies Proteins made by white blood cells as part of the body's immune system, to attack germs and help fight infection.

Bacteria Microscopic single-celled organisms, also called microbes or germs; some cause infection in the body, while others are "friendly" bacteria that live in the intestines and on the skin.

Blind spot The point at the back of the eye where nerves lining the retina collect and turn toward the brain; there are no light-sensitive cells at the blind spot, so it is unable to see.

Brain stem The lower part of the brain, found at the top of the spinal cord; it controls breathing, heart rate, and many other basic processes needed for survival.

Carbohydrate A component of food that the body converts to sugar (glucose) for energy.

Cardiovascular system The system that transports blood around the body, powered by the heart.

Cartilage Tough but flexible material that protects the ends of bones at joints; it also gives structure to body parts such as the nose, outer ear, and tubes in the lungs and throat.

Cell The body's building block; cells make all of the body's tissues and organs and do all of its basic jobs.

Cerebral cortex The highly folded, "wrinkly" outer part of the cerebrum (brain); made of gray matter, which carries out much of the information processing in the brain.

Cholesterol A chemical, made in the liver from fats in the food we eat, that is used to build cell walls; too much cholesterol in the blood can damage blood vessels and lead to heart problems.

Chyme A gloppy, creamy fluid that leaves the stomach and passes to the small intestine; it consists of pulpy half-digested food, gastric juices, and enzymes.

Cilia Microscopic hairlike structures that pulse to move liquids and particles along inside some parts of the body.

Coronary Anything to do with the arteries that supply the heart with blood.

Dairy products Milk, and foods that are made from milk, such as butter and cheese.

Dentin The dense material underneath a tooth's outer coating of enamel.

Digestive system The system of tubes that breaks down food and absorbs it into the body.

Embryo The name for a developing baby up to the eighth week.

Enamel The hard and glossy coating on a tooth.

Endocrine system The system that controls the body's internal environment, using chemical messengers called hormones.

Enzyme A protein that speeds up chemical reactions in the body.

Epiglottis A flap of cartilage in the back of the throat that stops food and liquid from getting into the lungs.

Fetus A developing baby from the eighth week until birth.

The body has more than 200 separate **joints**—the places where bones meet.

Genes Chemical instructions made of DNA and kept in the nucleus, or control center, of a cell; they hold information on how to build a human body.

Glucose A sugar that is the body's main energy source.

Gonads The sex organs (male or female).

Hepatic Anything to do with the liver.

Hormone A chemical messenger that carries a signal from one cell to another; hormones are released by glands and cells.

Immune system The defense system that protects the body from infection.

Intercostal muscles Muscles between the ribs that help with breathing.

Lactic acid A mildly toxic waste product made by muscles during heavy exercise (when not enough oxygen is getting to the muscles).

Lobe A rounded body part that often forms a section of a large organ such as the brain, liver, or lungs.

Lymph A clear fluid that surrounds all body cells.

Lymphatic system The body system that drains and transports lymph and works with the immune system to fight infection.

Meninges A series of protective layers surrounding the brain and spinal cord.

Mucus A slimy bodily fluid produced by the linings or coverings of organs.

Musculoskeletal system The load-bearing system that supports the body (skeleton) and pulls on it to move it around (muscles).

Nervous system The network of nerve cells and fibers that transmits information around the body as electrical pulses; made up of the central nervous system (brain and spinal cord)

and peripheral nervous system (sensory and motor nerves), as well as the autonomic nervous system, which operates automatic bodily functions.

Neuron A single nerve cell.

Nutrients Vital chemicals we get from food, needed for the body's smooth running and growth.

Osteocyte A bone-making cell.

Proteins A group of essential body chemicals that are used to build new tissues such as muscle fibers, hair, and nails; antibodies and enzymes are also proteins.

Pulmonary Anything to do with the lungs.

Renal Anything to do with the kidneys.

Reproductive system The body system that makes sex cells (sperm in males and eggs in females) and is in charge of making new humans.

Respiratory system The system in charge of breathing air—bringing fresh oxygen into the body and releasing waste carbon dioxide.

Sinus A cavelike opening in a bone that can often fill with fluid.

Sphincter A ring of muscle controlling an opening in the body—for example, in the anus or the bladder's outlet.

Synapse A structure that allows a neuron to pass on an electrical or chemical signal to another cell.

Urea A waste product from the breakdown of proteins in the body; removed in urine (pee).

Urinary system The system that filters waste and excess water from the blood and releases it from the body as urine (pee).

Viruses Tiny infectious agents, usually much smaller than bacteria, that multiply inside cells.